Our OHIO

Photography and text by Ian Adams

Voyageur Press

Edited by Kari Cornell
Designed by Julie Vermeer
Printed in China

04   05   06   07   08   5   4   3   2   1

Library of Congress Cataloging-in-Publication Data
Adams, Ian, 1946-
  Our Ohio / Ian Adams.
    p. cm.
  ISBN 0-89658-658-8 (hardback)
  1. Ohio—Pictorial works. I. Title.
  F492.A33 2004
  977.1'044'0222—dc22

                    2004012605

Distributed in Canada by Raincoast Books,
9050 Shaughnessy Street, Vancouver, B.C. V6P 6E5

Published by Voyageur Press, Inc.
123 North Second Street, P.O. Box 338,
Stillwater, MN 55082 U.S.A.
651-430-2210, fax 651-430-2211
books@voyageurpress.com
www.voyageurpress.com

Educators, fundraisers, premium and gift buyers, publicists, and marketing managers: *Looking for creative products and new sales ideas? Voyageur Press books are available at special discounts when purchased in quantities, and special editions can be created to your specifications. For details contact the marketing department at 800-888-9653.*

Frontispiece: *In spring dozens of waterfalls cascade along streams and over sandstone cliffs in the rugged Hocking Hills State Park in southeast Ohio near Logan.*

Page 2: *Redbud, dogwood, flowering maples and spring bulbs paint a tapestry of color in mid April at Kingwood Center, Ohio's most spectacular public garden, located near downtown Mansfield in Richland County.*

Page 3: *Adena, near Chilicothe in Ross County, was the home of Ohio's first governor and the father of Ohio's statehood, Thomas Worthington. The Buckeye State celebrated its bicentennial in 2003.*

Page 4: *The town square at Medina in northeast Ohio is surrounded by Victorian architecture, including the town hall, viewed here from the gazebo in the center of the square.*

Page 5, top: *Stern-wheelers line the banks of the Ohio River at Cincinnati during the Tall Stacks festival, part of the Ohio bicentennial celebrations in 2003.*

Page 5, bottom: *Residents of Chardon, a town in the northeastern part of the state, gather for a summer concert on the village green. (Photograph © Frank Kuchirchuk/The Image Finders)*

Title page: *The barn glows at sunrise on an Amish farm near Charm in Holmes County, in north-central Ohio, the heart of the state's largest Amish community.*

Title page, inset: *Shelf mushrooms and maple leaves create an abstract design in fall at Johnson Woods State Nature Preserve, near Orville in Wayne County. The preserve contains one of Ohio's largest stands of old-growth forest.*

Facing page: *Marblehead Lighthouse, built in 1821 from locally quarried limestone, is the oldest lighthouse still in use on the Great Lakes. The lighthouse stands sixty-seven feet above the rocks of Lake Erie at the entrance to Sandusky Bay in northwest Ohio.*

Below: *The Amish are primarily dairy farmers, and the large barn that typically forms the centerpiece of the Amish farm provides winter shelter for livestock.*

Above: *This field in Holmes County has become a graveyard for old tractors. Although some Mennonite farmers use tractors, the Amish prefer to use horses for most farming tasks.*

Left: *The Amish community in Holmes County is a major tourist attraction for the state. Visitors enjoy tours of the farms, purchase quilts and sturdy Amish furniture, and savor delicious meals prepared from locally grown livestock and produce.*

Above: *Amish buggies line a field at a barn raising in Holmes County. In Ohio the buggies are black, but in Amish communities in other states they are sometimes white, gray, or yellow.*

Amish children in central Ohio watch attentively as family and friends work together to build a barn. (Photograph © Jim Baron/The Image Finders)

Spectators watch a large Amish barn being "raised" in less than a day by Amish men from precut wooden beams and roofing materials. Wooden pegs, inserted into holes drilled by hand, brace the main barn structures.

Above: *An Amish farmer in Knox County transports hay from field to barn using horses and a wagon. (Photograph © Rita Byron/The Image Finders)*

Facing page: *Lupines add color to an Amish farm garden near Mount Hope in Holmes County. Most Amish farms also have an extensive vegetable garden and a few fruit trees.*

In the summertime, vegetable stands crop up along many roadsides in Amish country, offering fresh tomatoes, cucumbers, zucchini, green beans, honey, eggs, and handmade goods such as Amish dolls. This stand is near Middlefield. (Photograph © Carl A. Stimac/The Image Finders)

Above: *The Scarecrow Festival, held in Washington Court House the first weekend after Labor Day each year, features live music, a carnival, and a scarecrow contest. (Photograph © Jim Yokajty/The Image Finders)*

Right: *At the Slate Run Living Historical Farm near Columbus, a group of school children learn first hand what it took to run a farm in the 1880s. In addition to the gardens, the park also includes a fully restored home and barn from the period. (Photograph © Jeff Greenberg/The Image Finders)*

Above: *A winter snowfall creates a Currier and Ives landscape near New Bedford in Coshocton County on the edge of Ohio's largest Amish settlement area. After the hard work in the fields in spring, summer, and fall, the Amish spend the winter repairing tools and visiting with friends and family.*

Facing page: *Ice coats grasses and a fence near an old barn with triple cupolas near Bournville in Ross County. Ohio has fine examples of many types of barns, though sadly many have fallen victim to the ravages of time.*

Facing page: *Afternoon light illuminates Main Street at Zoar Village, a historic town in Tuscarawas County south of Canton. Founded by Joseph Bimeler in 1818, the community adopted communism and celibacy in an effort to survive religious persecution.*

Above: *Visitors to Zoar Village explore the town, stopping in the many shops that sell handmade candles, antiques, and primitive furniture, or grabbing a bite to eat at one of several good German restaurants for which the town is known. (Photograph © Jim Baron/The Image Finders)*

Above: *This elegant building in Marion is a memorial to President Warren Harding, an Ohioan who occupied the Oval Office from 1921 until 1923. Ohio is the birthplace of seven United States presidents, second only to Virginia.*

Facing page: *The knot garden is part of an extensive herb garden at Kingwood Center, established in Mansfield by local industrialist Charles King. Kingwood Center also features a conservatory, a rose garden, perennial and woodland gardens, and thousands of spring bulbs.*

Above: *Spring bulbs frame a view of the mansion at Kingwood Center, the home of industrialist Charles King. The twenty-six-acre public gardens at Kingwood Center are among Ohio's finest.*

Facing page: *The Longaberger corporate headquarters building near Newark is a seven-story replica of one of the company's well-known baskets. The structure weighs about 9,000 tons. The 150-ton handles are heated to prevent ice formation in winter.*

Above: *This thriving group of bald cypress can be found at Dawes Arboretum near Newark in Licking County. A boardwalk takes visitors into the cypress grove, enlivened by yellow iris in late spring.*

Left: *Millbrook Falls cascades over sandstone cliffs in a hollow framed with hemlock trees, located close to the scenic Kokosing River in Coshocton County.*

An Ohio Central Railroad steam-powered locomotive prepares to leave the Sugarcreek station for a trip through the Amish countryside. (Photograph © Jim Baron/The Image Finders)

The Red Brick Tavern was built in 1837 along the National Road, which ran through Ohio from Wheeling, West Virginia, to Indiana. The tavern, located west of Columbus in Lafayette, hosted six U.S. presidents.

Downtown Columbus, Ohio's largest city and the state capital, rises above the Olentangy River.

Above: *Mona Lisa's famous smile adorns this building in the Short North area of Columbus, a neighborhood filled with art galleries, restaurants, and boutiques. (Photograph © Jeff Greenberg/The Image Finders)*

Left: *A replica of Christopher Columbus's Santa Maria is permanently docked on the Scioto River in Battelle Riverfront Park, downtown Columbus. Visitors may tour the ship's interior. (Photograph © William Manning/The Image Finders)*

The Ohio State University band takes the field to entertain the crowd during halftime in a matchup with Northwestern University. The Ohio State Buckeyes football team is tremendously popular, and people travel to Columbus from all over the state to see the Big Ten team play. (Photograph © Wagner Photo/ The Image Finders)

A crowd gathers to watch jugglers play with fire at the Easton Town Center shopping mall in Columbus. (Photograph © Jeff Greenberg/The Image Finders)

Youngsters don tinsel wigs for fun at the Ohio State Fair. The fair, held each August in Columbus, is a summer highlight for many Ohioans. (Photograph © Jeff Greenberg/The Image Finders)

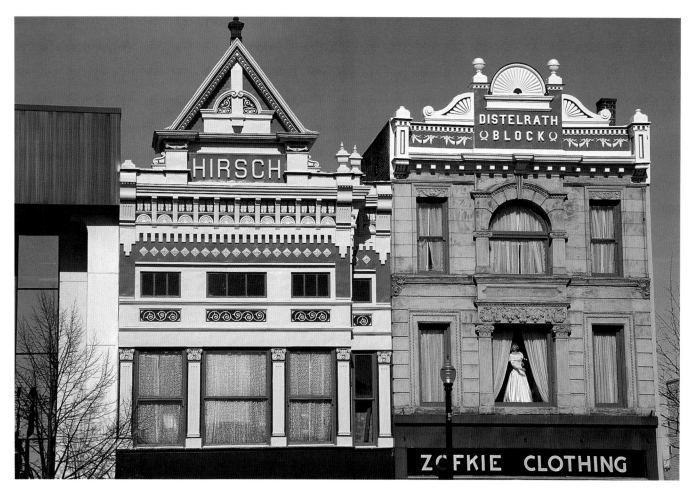

Above: *Turn-of-the-century ornamentation decorates build-ings in downtown Wapakoneta. The Shawnee and Seneca Indians lived in this area, which was the site of the first sawmill and gristmill in northwest Ohio.*

Right: *Neon lights adorn the façade of the Wapa Theater in Wapakoneta, located in northwest Ohio's Auglaize County. Nearby is the Neil Armstrong Air & Space Museum, honoring Wapakoneta's native son, astronaut, and moonwalker.*

Facing page: *Castle Piatt Mac-O-Chee is one of two Ohio castles built by two brothers a mile apart in a beautiful rural valley near West Liberty in Logan County. The Flemish-inspired castle was built in 1881 by Donn Piatt.*

Above: *Horace Duncan built this magnificent round barn in 1908 on the Manchester farm near New Hampshire in Auglaize County.*

Left: *Grain silos frame a bovine sculpture at Gilboa in rural Putnam County.*

Facing page: *Barn painter Scott Hagan was commissioned by The Ohio Bicentennial Commission to paint the Ohio Bicentennial Mural on one barn in each of Ohio's eighty-eight counties. This 1926 barn is in Defiance County.*

Above: *Spatterdock lilies bloom at Sheldon Marsh State Nature Preserve near Sandusky in Erie County. This is a popular staging area for birds on their northward migration across Lake Erie each spring.*

Left: *A misty sunrise gives a dreamlike quality to Killdeer Plains Wildlife Area near Upper Sandusky in Wyandot County. This 8,600-acre area of cropland, prairie remnants, woodlands, fields, and ponds is visited by thousands of ducks and geese in the spring, summer, and fall, and by short-eared owls in winter.*

The federal-style Wolcott House in Maumee is the headquarters of the Maumee Valley Historical Society and the Wolcott House Museum Complex, which includes a log home, a saltbox farmhouse, and other nineteenth-century buildings.

Wild lupine and yellow puccoon bloom in spring at Kitty Todd State Nature Preserve in the Oak Openings area west of Toledo. Lupine is the food plant of the endangered Karner Blue butterfly.

The view of downtown Toledo from International Park across the Maumee River is spectacular. Both Michigan and Ohio originally claimed the Toledo area, and it took an act of Congress in 1836 to settle the "Toledo War." Congress gave Toledo to Ohio and Michigan got the Upper Peninsula.

The S.S. Willis B. Boyer *was built in 1911 and "retired" in 1980 after sixty-nine years of service as a Great Lakes freighter. The 10,000-ton, 617-foot-long boat is now a freighter museum at International Park on the Maumee River at Toledo.*

Mark di Suvero's rubber and steel sculpture Blubber *stands in front of the Center for the Visual Arts at the Toledo Museum of Art. The zinc-coated copper building, designed by famed architect Frank Gehry, was completed in 1992.*

Above: *The Docks along the Maumee River in Toledo offers alfresco dining.*
(Photograph © Jeff Greenberg/The Image Finders)

Facing page: *Summertime brings mountains of fresh, colorful produce to the tables*
that line the Erie Street Market in Toledo's Warehouse District. (Photograph © Jeff
Greenberg/The Image Finders)

Toledo's historic West End District is home to the nation's largest community of late - Victorian homes. Many have been beautifully restored and the city offers walking tours of the area. (Photograph © Jeff Greenberg/The Image Finders)

Tony Packo's Café on Front Street in Toledo is a local landmark, made famous when actor and Toledo native Jamie Farr, who played Corporal Klinger on M*A*S*H*, raved about the restaurant's hot dogs. (Photograph © Jim Baron/The Image Finders)

Fort Meigs State Memorial, located along the Maumee River in Perrysburg, is the largest walled fort in the country. The fort was an important stronghold during the War of 1812, and interpreters reenact events from the conflict for visitors. (Photograph © Jeff Greenberg/The Image Finders)

An interpreter at Fort Meigs demonstrates the use of a hatchet to a tour group.
(Photograph © Jeff Greenberg/The Image Finders)

Above: *A visitor looks out over Lake Erie from the top of Marblehead Lighthouse, built in 1822. (Photograph © Jeff Greenberg/The Image Finders)*

Facing page: *The Marblehead Lighthouse stands sixty-five feet above the limestone rocks of Lake Erie. The lighthouse was renovated and became an Ohio state park in 1998.*

Above: *Slabs of ice line the shore under the Marblehead Lighthouse in late winter. In hard winters, more than a foot of ice covers sections of western Lake Erie.*

Facing page: *Sunrise lights up the ice at Marblehead near Port Clinton. Ice fishing is a popular winter activity in this area, and ice shanties are a common sight on frozen Lake Erie. Ice fisherman primarily catch perch and walleye.*

Below: *Father and daughter enjoy a ride on Kimberly's Antique Carousel in the resort town of Put-in-Bay on South Bass Island. The handcarved wooden horses, dogs, and other animals date from 1917. (Photograph © Jeff Greenberg/The Image Finders)*

Above: *In the summer, the population of South Bass Island swells from just under 500 to 1,500. These two young tourists cool off with tasty ice cream cones. (Photograph © Jim Baron/The Image Finders)*

Facing page: *Perry's Victory and International Peace Memorial rises 352 feet over Lake Erie and the town of Put-in-Bay. The monument, completed in 1915, commemorates Oliver H. Perry's victory over the British in the War of 1812. (Photograph © Carl A. Stimac/The Image Finders)*

The Wileswood Country Store in the Lake Erie town of Huron has been selling candy in the style of an old New England general store since the 1890s. (Photograph © Jeff Greenberg/The Image Finders)

A vintner checks the clarity of a batch of wine in the barrel fermentation room of Sandusky's Firelands Winery. Firelands, in business since 1880, is the largest winery along Lake Erie. (Photograph © Jeff Greenberg/The Image Finders)

Above: *The tallest cliffs along Lake Erie are on Gibraltar Island in Put-in-Bay on South Bass Island. From these cliffs, Commodore Perry reputedly kept watch for the English fleet that he would later defeat in the Battle of Lake Erie on September 10, 1813.*

Facing page: *This lighthouse stands near Lake Erie at the Inland Seas Maritime Museum in Vermilion. The lighthouse is a replica of the original 1847 lighthouse, and stands in front of the Wakefield Mansion, headquarters of the Great Lakes Historical Society.*

Inventor Thomas Alva Edison was born in this small brick house in Milan on February 11, 1847. Several of his inventions are on display in the house and adjoining museum.

This magnificent stand of large white trillium, Ohio's state wildflower, grows in a small woodland near Milan in Erie County.

Above: *Headlands Dunes State Nature Preserve is one of the few remaining beach and dune natural areas along the south shore of Lake Erie. The preserve is located in Lake County near Mentor.*

Right: *The Fairport Harbor West Breakwater Lighthouse, built in 1925, is located at the mouth of the Grand River in Lake County, midway between Cleveland and Ashtabula.*

NO TRESPASSING
PROPERTY OF
U.S. GOVERNMENT
VIOLATORS
WILL BE
PROSECUTED

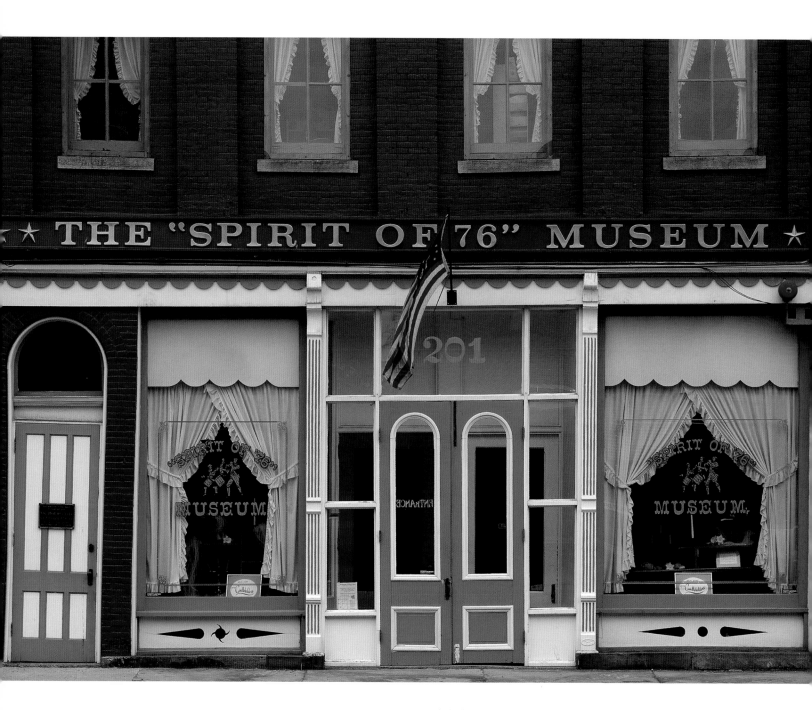

Archibald Willard, famous for his patriotic painting The Spirit of '76, *is celebrated at this museum in Wellington.*

Buildings line the streets of downtown Mansfield in Richland County.

Above: *A young 4-H member visits with the Holstein cow he's showing at the Geauga County Fair in Burton. (Photograph © Jim Baron/The Image Finders)*

Left: *Riders young and old enjoy a spin on the colorful carousel at the Lorain County Fair in Wellington. (Photograph © Carl A. Stimac/The Image Finders)*

Facing page: *The bright lights of the midway blur against the evening sky at the Geauga County Fair, the oldest fair in the state. (Photograph © Carl A. Stimac/The Image Finders)*

Right: *The Key Tower and Terminal Tower are two of the tallest buildings in downtown Cleveland.*

Below: *Rhododendrons and a waterfall provide tranquility and beauty at Cleveland Botanical Garden in University Circle on Cleveland's east side.*

The lakefront at the end of East Ninth Street offers an excellent view of the Cleveland skyline. The Rock and Roll Hall of Fame is shown on the left.

The ultra-modern Rock and Roll Hall of Fame and Museum opened in late 1995 and has been a Cleveland hot spot ever since. The glass pyramid, designed by I. M. Pei, is the center of the hall of fame, where rock's legends have been enshrined. (Photograph © Jim Baron/The Image Finders)

The colorful 1939 International Harvester bus that Ken Kesey and the Merry Pranksters drove across the country in the psychedelic 60s is now permanently parked at the Rock and Roll Hall of Fame. (Photograph © Jim Baron/The Image Finders)

Above: *Renovated shops and restaurants in Cleveland's Warehouse District attract shoppers and residents to the area. In 1982, the century-old neighborhood was listed on the National Register of Historic Places. (Photograph © Jim Baron/The Image Finders)*

Facing page: *Cleveland's Italian residents celebrate the Feast of the Assumption each August with religious parades through the Little Italy neighborhood, good food, and wine. (Photograph © Jim Baron/The Image Finders)*

Above: *A group performs music for the crowd at Culture Fest, a celebration of African American culture held each year at Forest City Park in East Cleveland. The festival typically features food, games, and crafts. (Photograph © Jim Baron/The Image Finders)*

Above: *Cleveland Browns fans take their team and the stadium's famous Dawg Pound very seriously. (Photograph © Jim Baron/The Image Finders)*

Right: *After the original Cleveland Browns moved to Baltimore at the end of the 1995 season, the fans were outraged. The city struck a deal with the NFL to build a new stadium. The stadium, shown here in 1999, the year it opened, became the new home of an expansion team aptly named the Cleveland Browns. (Photograph © Jim Baron/The Image Finders)*

On weekends during the holiday season, Manner's Pine Tree Lodge in Ashtabula offers horse-drawn wagon rides to customers who come to cut their own tree. (Photograph © Jim Baron/The Image Finders)

A late winter snowfall brightens this view of Corning Lake, part of the Holden Arboretum in Lake and Geauga Counties. Holden is one of America's largest arboretums, with 3,300 acres of woodlands, streams and ponds, meadows, ravines, and horticultural collections.

Right: *At Gorge Metro Park, located just outside of Akron, outdoor enthusiasts hike one of the rustic trails that cuts through the sandstone cliffs carved long ago by the Cuyahoga River.*

Below: *Tupelo leaves create an abstract pattern on the moss at Thompson Ledges Park in Ashtabula County.*

Facing page: *Phelps Creek runs through a cliff-lined ravine at Warner Hollow in Ashtabula County near Windsor. The hollow is a refuge for wildflowers, birds, and at least eight species of salamanders.*

Above: *The Herrick House is part of Hale Farm and Village, a reconstruction of an 1830s rural community in Ohio's Western Reserve. It is located in the Cuyahoga Valley National Park between Cleveland and Akron.*

Right: *Cascade Falls tumbles over cliffs of Berea sandstone near downtown Elyria in Lorain County.*

Facing page: *An early morning mist covers the lake at Frame Lake/Herrick Fen State Nature Preserve in Portage County north of Kent.*

Above: *Christ Church Museum at Windsor in Ashtabula County is in the heart of northeast Ohio's Western Reserve, an area with architecture reminiscent of New England.*

Left: *Fishermen try their luck at Mogadore Reservoir in Portage County east of Akron. Mogadore is an excellent place to fish for bluegill, largemouth bass, and crappie.*

Above: *Football fans make special trips to the Pro Football Hall of Fame in Canton, Ohio, where they can tour one hundred years of pro football history in autographs, uniforms, and Super Bowl rings. (Photograph © Jim Baron/The Image Finders)*

Facing page: *The winning car crosses the finish line at the annual All-American Soap Box Derby race in Akron, Ohio. The race, held each July, gives young participants a chance to compete for scholarships and prizes. (Photograph © Jim Baron/ The Image Finders)*

Leafy and green, Goodyear Heights Metropolitan Park is a great place for a stroll on a lazy Sunday morning. The park is part of the planned community developed in the early 1900s by Goodyear Tire and Rubber founder Charles Goodyear, who wanted to provide employees with a pleasant place to live within walking distance of the plant. (Photograph © Jim Baron/The Image Finders)

Founded in 1870 as Buchtel College, Akron University provides a quality education in the heart of the city. (Photograph © Jim Baron/The Image Finders)

Above: *The Wheeling-Pittsburgh steel plant is framed by the Ohio River at Mingo Junction in Jefferson County. This gritty area, part of Ohio's "rust belt," was the setting for the 1978 movie* The Deer Hunter *starring Robert De Niro and Meryl Streep.*

Facing page: *This octagonal barn, one of about thirty round and polygonal barns remaining in the Buckeye State, stands near Piedmont in rural Harrison County.*

Above: *Hills covered bridge is one of five covered bridges along Route 26 east of Marietta in Washington and Monroe Counties. This picturesque rural road is often called Ohio's Covered Bridge Highway.*

Facing page: *The Magnolia Flouring Mill stands along the Sandy & Beaver Canal in the town of Magnolia in Stark County.*

Above: *Longhorn cattle graze the hills on the Dickinson Cattle Company ranch near Barnesville.*

Facing page: *Legendary barn painter Harley Warrick painted this Mail Pouch mural on a barn near Route 78 in Morgan County. Warrick painted or repainted more than 25,000 barns during his long career.*

Above: *Clendening Lake in Harrison County is one of several large lakes created in the mid 1900s by the Muskingum Watershed Conservancy in a region once sorely abused by strip mining, but now popular for fishing and other recreational activities.*

Right: *Evening falls near Salt Fork State Park in Guernsey County. Salt Fork is the largest of the seventy-four state parks in the Buckeye State.*

Below: *Erwin Hall, completed in 1850 in the federal style, is the oldest building on the campus of Marietta College in Washington County.*

Above: Mound Cemetery in Marietta is named for the Indian mound shown in the photograph. Reputedly there are more Revolutionary War officers buried here than in any other place in the country.

Facing page: The picturesque Dickerson Church is located in the hill country near Cadiz in rural Harrison County.

In early fall, the Ohio Stern-Wheeler Festival draws vintage stern-wheelers to Marietta, Ohio's first settlement. Marietta was founded in 1788 and named for Queen Marie Antoinette as thanks to France for its help in America's Revolutionary War.

Above: *Cutler Hall, built in 1816 in the federal style, is Ohio's oldest college building. It faces the Green, the heart of the attractive campus at Ohio University in Athens.*

Above: *A guide in Victorian dress gives walking tours of the historic Ohio River town of Pomeroy. (Photograph © Jeff Greenberg/The Image Finders)*

Zanesville was founded in 1799 by pioneer Ebenezer Zane, who cut the first road, Zane's Trace, through the Ohio Wilderness. From 1810 until 1812, Zanesville was Ohio's state capital.

Above: *These murals, painted on the east wall of a bank building in Pomeroy, display historic scenes of Meigs County.*

Facing page: *The Jewel Evans Grist Mill is located in Gallia County, home of restaurant founder and farmer Bob Evans.*

Rose Hollow Falls is one of dozens of seasonal waterfalls found in the Hocking Hills State Park, south of Logan in Hocking County. Some of Ohio's most scenic hiking trails run through this rugged area.

Above: *Conkle's Hollow State Nature Preserve includes the Rim Trail, an exciting two-mile hike along the rim of sandstone cliffs more than one hundred feet high that line the east and west sides of the hollow. This photo was taken from the East Rim.*

Above: *Canter's Cave is a rugged area of woodlands and sandstone cliffs in Jackson County.*

Above: *A misty spring morning reveals woodland abstracts along a dirt road in Shawnee State Forest west of Portsmouth.*

Left: *Virginia Bluebells bloom along a stream at Lake Katharine State Nature Preserve near Jackson. This large preserve is also home to a few timber rattlesnakes as well as rare trees and plants.*

Facing page: *Sandstone cliffs reach more than two hundred feet at Conkle's Hollow State Nature Preserve in the scenic Hocking Hills State Park.*

Above: *Ohio buckeyes, the inedible nuts produced by the state tree of the same name, are believed to bring good luck. (Photograph © Jim Baron/The Image Finders)*

Facing page: *Ullysses S. Grant was born in this Point Pleasant cabin in 1822. Despite his prowess as a general in the Civil War, Grant proved to be an undistinguished U.S. president and teetered on the edge of bankruptcy toward the end of his life. Grant died of throat cancer in 1885.*

Facing page: *The Roebling Suspension Bridge, which spans the Ohio River between Cincinnati and Newport, Kentucky, was opened in 1866. At that time the 1,057-foot main span was the world's longest.*

Left: *Downtown Cincinnati and the north tower of the Roebling Suspension Bridge frame the Mike Fink stern-wheeler restaurant in Newport, Kentucky.*

Below: *The sun rises above Over-the-Rhine, an area north of downtown Cincinnati. Settled by German immigrants during the second half of the nineteenth century, this area has the nation's largest collection of Italianate architecture.*

Above: *The Temple of Love, built in 1845, is the only remaining building from Cincinnatian Robert Bowler's Mount Storm estate.*

Left: *Ohio has many murals, but without doubt the most spectacular is the Cincinnatus mural, by Robert Haas, a splendid trompe l'oeil that covers the north side of the Cincinnatus Building in downtown Cincinnati.*

Facing page: *The magnificent Union Terminal in Cincinnati is one of America's finest examples of art deco design. The building, constructed in 1933 as a train station, is now a museum center.*

Above: *The Great American Ballpark was christened the new home for the Cincinnati Reds during the team's opening game against the Pittsburgh Pirates in 2003. The tall stacks of a stern-wheeler are incorporated into the bleacher seat area, paying homage to the stadium's location on the mighty Ohio River. (Photograph © Tom Uhlman/The Image Finders)*

Facing page: *Stern-wheelers are stacked along the Ohio River at the Tall Stacks festival, part of Ohio's 2003 bicentennial celebrations in Cincinnati, the Queen City.*

Right: *Bear's Mill, located in Darke County, is one of a handful of operating grist mills remaining in the Buckeye State. Gabriel Baer built the mill in 1849.*

Below: *This old mill is located near Yellow Springs in Greene County on the banks of the scenic Little Miami River.*

Facing page: *Clifton Mill, one of the largest grist mills ever built in the United States, is located along the Little Miami River in the village of Clifton in Greene County.*

Above: *School children enjoy a ride in a Turtle Creek Valley Railway 1930s coach car. The trains leave from the station in Lebanon and carry passengers on a fourteen-mile round trip through the surrounding countryside. (Photograph © Jeff Greenberg/The Image Finders)*

Facing page: *The Lane-Hooven House, built in Hamilton in 1863, is a superb example of an octagonal, Victorian Gothic building.*

Above: *Antioch Hall at Antioch College is framed by redbud in early spring. The college is located in Greene County at Yellow Springs.*

Facing page: *The McKinley Birthplace Memorial was built in 1917 at Niles in Warren County. President William McKinley served in the Oval Office from 1896 until September 6, 1901, when he was assassinated in Buffalo, New York.*

Above: *A colorfully restored railroad bridge marks the entrance to Dayton's Oregon Historic District, the city's oldest neighborhood, dating from 1829. A neighborhood revitalization project begun thirty years ago has made Oregon the ideal place to shop, dine, or just relax. (Photograph © Jim Yokajty/ The Image Finders)*

Left: *A young actor in period costume stands with a vintage bicycle in front of the Wright Brothers' shop and museum in Dayton Aviation Heritage National Historic Park. Aviation enthusiasts can see one of the brothers' famous airplanes, the 1905 Wright Flyer III, in the park's Carillon area. (Photograph © Jim Yokajty/The Image Finders)*

Facing page: *A vibrant hot-air balloon attracted attention at Dayton's Rally by the River in 1998, an event held to generate interest in a riverfront renovation project. The result has been Riverscape, a park along the Great Miami River that features a landscape garden, bike paths and walkways, a fountain and light show, and more. (Photograph © Jim Yokajty/The Image Finders)*

Above: *The Shelby County courthouse was built in 1881 and is the centerpiece of the town square in downtown Sydney. The Second Empire–style courthouse, built of limestone and sandstone, has a central tower and four corner towers.*

Facing page: *The People's Federal Savings & Loan Bank of Sydney in Shelby County is one of eight Midwestern banks designed by Louis Sullivan, a pioneer of American architecture. The Sydney bank, which was Sullivan's favorite, was built in 1917.*

Above: *Charleston Falls Preserve is in the village of West Charleston in Greene County. The stream plummets thirty-seven feet over limestone cliffs on its way to join the Great Miami River one mile to the west.*

Facing page: *A waterfall carries Sharon Creek over limestone rocks in Sharon Creek State Nature Preserve, north of Cincinnati in Hamilton County.*

Sycamore trees line the banks of Caesar Creek at Caesar Creek State Nature Preserve in Warren County. Numerous species of wildflowers fill the woods here in early spring.